Tract...
& R...

Burrell of Thetford

Contents

Introduction	2
Ploughing engines	3
Road rollers	5
Road locomotives	9
Gold Medal Tractors	15
Traction engines	18
Showman's road locomotives and tractors	38

Frontispiece: The Burrell emblem, photographed on an engine at the St Agnes Rally in August 1992.

First published in 2011
British Library Cataloguing in Publication Data
A catalogue record for this book is available from the British Library.

ISBN 978 1 85794 378 8

Introduction

Charles Burrell & Sons Ltd was a builder of very high-quality, reliable road steam engines. The firm can be traced back to 1770, when Joseph Burrell opened a smithy in St Nicholas Street, Thetford, Norfolk, originally repairing agricultural equipment, then making his own farming equipment. The smithy eventually expanded to become the St Nicholas Works, producing a whole range of agricultural equipment renowned for its workmanship, an ethos that continued throughout the life of the firm.

Charles was a popular first name at Burrells, as three directors carried that name; the first, who became Works Manager, saw the company through the glory years of the 19th century. In the 1840s the first portables were designed. A decade and a half later the company produced its first self-propelled traction engine; previously, as with the products of most of the other engineering firms, steam engines had been hauled by horses to their place of work, so this was a major step forward in traction engine design. Burrell was always keen to advance its designs, and in the 1870s was one of the first companies to fit solid rubber tyres to its road steam locomotives.

Burrell diversified in the late 19th century, producing not only agricultural equipment like threshing machines, which had always been part of its portfolio, but also steam launches, marine engines and steam tram engines, among others. Steam road rollers were produced from the 1890s, followed a decade later by the company's superbly finished showman's road locomotives and tractors, very well liked by the fairground operators because of their build quality. In 1908 Burrell won the RAC-sponsored steam tractor trials for light haulage, and was awarded a Gold Medal; henceforth these engines were known as Gold Medal Tractors. Just before the First World War, Burrell introduced a steam wagon.

In the 1920s Burrell joined the consortium called Agricultural & General Engineers Ltd, which, when it collapsed in 1932, took this illustrious firm with it. Some 330 engines of all types are in preservation in this country, including two ploughing engines from 1879, which are kept at the Museum of East Anglian Life at Stowmarket. The Charles Burrell Museum in Minstergate, Thetford, records the history of the firm, and has many exhibits on show including a display of engines.

Silver Link Publishing Ltd
The Trundle
Ringstead Road
Great Addington
Kettering
Northants NN14 4BW

Tel/Fax: 01536 330588
email: sales@nostalgiacollection.com
Website: www.nostalgiacollection.com

Printed and bound in Česká Republika

Ploughing engines

WEETING Seen at the July 2002 rally is an 1879 Burrell ploughing engine, one of a preserved pair called *The Countess* and *The Earl*.

WEETING At the same rally back in July 1996, the ploughing engine brings in the plough. These two ploughing engines are the second and third oldest known preserved examples.

Road rollers

Left: WEETING 1912 Burrell 12½-ton road roller *Jeanette* in action at the May 2008 rally.

Above: **ASTLE PARK** 1913 10-ton road roller *Old Ernie* was photographed at the Astle Park Rally in August 1994.

PORTHTOWAN During the West of England Steam Engine Society road run in Cornwall in August 1995, 1924 10-ton road roller *Ernie* tops Engine Hill.

TARRANT HINTON A visitor to the Great Dorset Steam Fair in September 2002 is this 1925 8-ton road roller.

ROXTON With this former rally in the background, we see 1926 10-ton road roller *Heather* in September 1993.

Road locomotives

STONELEIGH PARK The Stoneleigh Park Country Show is no longer held, but back in August 1991 1912 Burrell road locomotive *The Dalesman* was one of the visitors.

GOVERS HILL The West of England Steam Engine Society Road Run in Cornwall in August 1995 also featured 1911 Burrell road locomotive *Clinker*.

BELVOIR CASTLE The same engine is seen again nine years later at the Belvoir Castle Rally of May 2004.

Above: **LEONARD STANLEY** Pausing
during a local club road run at Leonard Stanley,
near Stroud, Gloucestershire, is 1919 road
locomotive *Lord Fisher of Lambeth*.

Left: **ST AGNES** Passing an assorted line-up
of engines at the St Agnes Rally in Cornwall
in August 1992 is 1924 road locomotive
Conqueror.

BANBURY Leading this pair of Burrells at the Banbury Rally of June 2004 is 1931 road locomotive *Dorothy*, an engine that was actually built by Garrett.

TARRANT HINTON Heavy Haulage on the Hill: leading this procession of engines at the Great Dorset Steam Fair in September 2003 is 1914 Burrell road locomotive *Duke of Kent*.

Gold Medal Tractors

STOKE ROW The Burrell Gold Medal Tractor was so called because it won the Gold Medal in the 1905 RAC trials, and was a much sought after engine in its heyday, as it still is today. At the Stoke Row Rally we see 1912 tractor *Charlie*.

Above: **APPLEFORD** Outside The Carpenters Arms at Appleford, Oxfordshire, in July 2006 is 1913 Burrell tractor *May Queen*. The Carpenters Arms and Appleford were the birthplace of today's preservation scene 60 years ago and the now famous 'wager for ale' by Arthur Napper, which arguably started the traction engine movement.

Right: **LANGPORT** The 1913 tractor *Defiance* is seen at this Somerset rally in July 2006.

WADDESDON Self-advertising 1927 Gold Medal Tractor *Tinkerbell* took part in the Waddesdon Rally in September 1992. This rally is no longer held.

Traction engines

ROXTON In July 1991 this one-time rally was host to 1877 Burrell traction engine *Century*, the oldest known Burrell in preservation.

WEETING At the Weeting Rally in July 1998 is 1886 traction engine *Maria*, belted to a rare Burrell threshing drum. Like most firms, Burrell made not only engines but also many agricultural and other engineering products, such as threshing machines.

WEETING With agricultural equipment in tow, 1891 traction engine *The Old Chap* is at work at Fengate Farm, Weeting, in May 2008.

Left: **PORTHTOWAN** Another view of Engine Hill, Porthtowan, during the August 1995 West of England Steam Engine Society run. The engine is an 1895 Burrell.

Above: **OLD WARDEN** Posing outside Shuttleworth House during the Bedfordshire Steam Rally of September 2003 is 1898 traction engine *Old Lytham*.

BEAMISH In the yard of the re-created railway station at Beamish Open Air Museum in May 2008 is 1898 traction engine *The Duke of Ongar*.

WEETING A threshing scene from the days of steam at Fengate Farm in May 2008. The engine is an 1899 traction engine.

Top left: **WELLAND** This rally is held at Welland, between Upton-on-Severn and Malvern, and in July 2008 1901 traction engine *Old Duch* steams by; the Malvern Hills can be seen in the background.

Left: **HATTON** A farmyard scene at a National Traction Engine Trust Training Weekend held at Hatton Country World. The engine is 1901 engine *Ted Haggard*.

Above: **ONSLOW PARK** 1902 Burrell traction engine *General C. R. deWet* poses at the Salop Rally of August 1994.

Right: **OLD WARDEN** 1903 traction engine *Spitfire/Delarey* is seen at the Bedfordshire Steam Rally in September 2003, with Shuttleworth House once more providing the backdrop.

Left: **WEETING** At Fengate Farm in May 2008 *Spitfire/Delarey* works for its living demonstrating stone crushing.

Opposite: **PORTHTOWAN** Back to Engine Hill, overlooking Porthtowan, during the West of England Steam Engine Society run of August 1995; 1907 traction engine *Little Mac* breasts the climb.

Top left: **MUCH MARCLE** *Little Mac* is seen again at the Marcle Rally in July 2006.

Left: **WEETING** 1907 traction engine *Dreadnought* hauls a Marshall threshing drum and elevator at Fengate Farm in May 2008.

Above: **WEETING** The same engine plays its role in an authentic threshing scene from the steam age at the July 1999 rally.

FROCESTER On a local club road in Gloucestershire in May 2004, a 1907 'Aberdeenshire'-type traction engine and a 1912 Burrell traction engine are at rest.

TIRLEY On a local road run at Tirley, south of Tewkesbury, Gloucestershire, two 1909 Burrell traction engines hauling re-creations of road trains pass the camera: *Keeling (opposite)* and *Victory (below)*.

Above: **WEETING** For a couple of years at the turn of the 21st century New Zealand Burrells visited their birthplace; hauling logs at the July 2002 rally is one of them, a 1909 engine.

WELLAND RALLY At Welland in July 2001 is another New Zealand Burrell, also with felled trees in tow, this time a 1913 traction engine.

Inset right: **WEETING** Also on logging duties, at Fengate Farm in May 2008, is 1915 crane traction engine *Lord Derby*.

GOVERS HILL Another picture taken during the West of England Steam Engine Society run in August 1995 shows 1919 traction engine *Cornish Maid* with showman's fittings.

DENNINGTON Joining the A1120 at Dennington during an East Anglian road run is 1922 traction engine *Jessie*.

NORTH NIBLEY At the Lister Tyndale Rally in Gloucestershire in June 2004 we see 1922 traction engine *Susie*. North Nibley church is in the background.

BIRMINGHAM Taking part in a road run through the Jewellery Quarter in Birmingham is 1922 traction engine *Janet*. The location is Brook Street, not far from Snow Hill station. This road run was discontinued in the mid-1990s.

ASTON CLINTON Roading through the village en route to the Chilterns Hills Rally is 1925 traction engine *Santon, IOM*.

ROXTON In September 1991 the appropriately named 1927 traction engine *Crimson Lady* is seen at this former rally.

WEETING 1930 traction engine *Rosemarie* attends the July 1996 rally.

Showman's road locomotives and tractors

Left: **LEIGHTON BUZZARD** In appropriate surroundings 1907 showman's tractor *Reliance* is seen at the Leighton Buzzard Rally in June 1996; this event is now known as the St Albans Rally.

Above: **WEARNE** 1909 showman's road locomotive *Gladiator* passes through Wearne, Somerset, during the Langport Rally road run in July 2005.

Above: **LINCOLNSHIRE RALLY** A striking portrait of 1911 showman's road locomotive *The Bailie* taken in August 1999.

Below: **CASTLEMORTON COMMON** On a road run to the Welland Rally, with the Malverns in the background and re-creating a showman's road train, is 1911 Burrell showman's road locomotive *Nancy*.

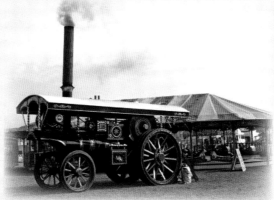

Above: **WELLAND RALLY** *Nancy* is seen again at the rally, which is justly famous for its collection of showman's engines and its re-creation of fairground scenes.

Left: **OLD WARDEN** At work in the fairground at the Bedfordshire Steam Rally in September 2004 is 1911 showman's road locomotive *Princess Mary*.

GOVERS HILL Back at Govers Hill on the August 1995 West of England Steam Engine Society road run we see 1912 showman's road locomotive *Star*.

NORTH ASTON Taking part in a local Oxfordshire road run in June 2004 is 1913 showman's road locomotive *King George VI*.

BELVOIR CASTLE A striking portrait of *His Lordship*, a 1913 showman's road locomotive at the May 2004 Belvoir Castle Rally.

OLD WARDEN Shuttleworth House is once again the backdrop for a portrait taken during the Bedfordshire Steam Rally of September 2003, showing 1915 showman's road locomotive *Nero* and its trailer, representing 'Bostock & Wombwell's Wonderful Performing Animals'.

WELLAND RALLY A pair of 1920 Burrell showman's road locomotives at the July 2002 Welland Rally: *Starlight* (left) and *Princess Mary.*

WELLAND RALLY Another showman's engine at the Welland Rally, this time 1921 road locomotive *St Brannock* with showman's fittings in July 2000.

WALSALL ARBORETUM At 'Pat Collins 150', commemorating the famous Midlands showman, in August 2009 is 1921 showman's road locomotive *Wait & See* (in original yellow livery), with 1916 Foster equivalent *Admiral Beatty* in the background.

NORTH NIBLEY At the Lister Tyndale Rally in June 2006 is 1925 traction engine *Supreme* with showman's fittings, demonstrating the blurring between the various types of engine.

Index

Build dates
1877 18
1879 2, 3
1886 19
1891 19
1895 20
1898 20, 21
1899 22
1901 23
1902 23
1903 24
1905 15
1907 24, 26, 27, 38
1909 29, 38
1911 10, 39
1912 5, 9, 15, 27, 40
1913 5, 16, 30, 41, 42
1914 14
1915 30, 43
1916 46
1919 12, 31
1920 44
1921 45, 46
1922 32, 33, 34
1924 6, 12
1925 7, 35, 47, 48
1926 8
1927 17, 36
1931 13

Engine names
Admiral Beatty 46
Century 18
Charlie 15
Clinker 10
Conqueror 12
Cornish Maid 31
Crimson Lady 36
Defiance 16
Dorothy 13
Dreadnought 26
Duke of Kent 14
Ernie 5, 6
Ex-Mayor 48

General C. R. deWet 23
Gladiator 38
Heather 8
His Lordship 42
Janet 34
Jeanette 5
Keeling 29
King George VI 41
Little Mac 24
Lord Derby 30
Lord Fisher of Lambeth
    12
Maria 19
May Queen 16
Nancy 39
Old Duch 23
Old Ernie 5
Old Lytham 20
Princess Mary 39, 44
Reliance 38
Rosemarie 37
Santon, IOM 35
Spitfire/Delarey 24
Star 40
Starlight 44
St Brannock 45
Supreme 47
Susie 33
Ted Haggard 23
The Bailie 39
The Countess 3
The Dalesman 9
The Duke of Ongar 21
The Earl 3
The Old Chap 19
Tinkerbell 17
Victory 29
Wait & See 46

Image dates
July 1991 18
August 1991 9
September 1991 36
August 1992 2, 12

September 1992 17
September 1993 8
August 1994 5, 23
August 1995 6, 10, 20,
    24, 31, 40
June 1996 38
July 1996 4, 37
July 1998 19
July 1999 26
August 1999 39
July 2000 45
July 2001 30
July 2002 3, 29, 44
September 2002 7
May 2003 48
September 2003 14, 20,
    24, 43
May 2004 11, 27, 42
June 2004 13, 33, 41
September 2004 39
July 2005 38
June 2006 47
July 2006 16, 26
July 2008 23
May 2008 5, 19, 21, 22,
    24, 26, 30
August 2009 46

Locations
APPLEFORD 16
ASTLE PARK 5
ASTON CLINTON 35
BANBURY 13
BEAMISH 21
BELVOIR CASTLE 11,
    42
BIRMINGHAM 34
CASTLEMORTON
    COMMON 39
DENNINGTON 32
FROCESTER 27
GAMLINGAY 48
GOVERS HILL 10, 31, 40
HATTON 23

LANGPORT 16

LEIGHTON BUZZARD
    38
LEONARD STANLEY
    12
LINCOLNSHIRE RALLY
    39
MUCH MARCLE 26
NORTH ASTON 41
NORTH NIBLEY 33, 47
OLD WARDEN 20, 24,
    39, 43
ONSLOW PARK 23
PORTHTOWAN 6,
    20, 24
ROXTON 8, 18, 36
ST AGNES 2, 12
STOKE ROW 15
STONELEIGH PARK 9
TARRANT HINTON
    7, 14
TIRLEY 29
WADDESDON 17
WALSALL ARBORETUM
    46
WEARNE 38
WEETING 3, 4, 5, 19, 22,
    24, 26, 29, 30, 37
WELLAND RALLY 30,
    39, 44, 45

GAMLINGAY Photographed during a Bedfordshire Club road run at Gamlingay village in May 2003 is 1925 showman's road locomotive *Ex-Mayor*.

Traction Engines
& Recollections

Fowler of Leeds

Contents

Introduction   2
Road locomotives   3
Road rollers   8
Traction engines   15
Showman's road locomotives   20
Ploughing engines   27

Frontispiece
TARRANT HINTON 1931 Fowler wagon
Pendle Prince at the Great Dorset Steam Fair in
September 1994 .

© Malcolm Ranieri, 2011

Photos: © Malcolm Ranieri, 2011 unless otherwise credited.

First published in 2011
British Library Cataloguing in Publication Data
A catalogue record for this book is available from the
British Library.

ISBN 978 1 85794 380 1
Silver Link Publishing Ltd

Introduction

The firm of John Fowler & Co is synonymous
with steam ploughing, and its mighty ploughing
engines dominated this form of mechanised
agriculture throughout the latter part of the
19th century and well into the first couple
of decades of the 20th before the ubiquitous
internal combustion engine took over in the
shape of the tractor.

The founder, John Fowler, was a mechanical
engineer specialising in agriculture, especially at
first land drainage. In 1857 he invented his first
self-moving ploughing engine, built by Clayton
& Shuttleworth. By 1862, however, John Fowler
was occupying his own engineering premises,
the Steam Plough Works in Leeds, Yorkshire.
Tragedy struck two years later when John
Fowler died in an accident, but his family and
business partners, especially a Scottish farmer
called David Greig, carried on the work. Almost
immediately portables and agricultural traction
engines were being built at the works. From
the 1880s onwards into the 20th century, in
addition to the ploughing engines and dedicated
ploughs, harrows and drainage equipment,
which sold all over the world, the company
also made steam road rollers, road locomotives
and showman's engines, wagons (from the mid-
1920s) and light haulage tractors.

The firm also diversified into the building
of stationary engines, railway locomotives,
colliery equipment, electricity generators
and machinery for local authorities. Fowlers
also exported, and established overseas
subsidiaries where the company's products
were built under licence. The firm managed
the downturn in steam products better than
most after the First World War, due in part
to a loyal customer base and diversification
into other forms of heavy engineering, and its
last steam engine, a road roller, was sold in
1937. Just prior to that, up to 1934, six 'Super
Lion' showman's road locomotives, considered
by some to be the pinnacle of road steam
engineering, were built.

The firm was taken over in 1947 by the T.
W. Ward Group, and Fowler as an individual
brand was no more. Approximately 700 Fowler
engines have been preserved, a quarter of
which are ploughing engines.

The Trundle
Ringstead Road
Great Addington
Kettering
Northants NN14 4BW
Tel/Fax: 01536 330588

email: sales@nostalgiacollection.com
Website: www.nostalgiacollection.com

Printed and bound in Česká Republika

PORTHTOWAN Photographed during the West of England Steam Engine Society's road run in August 1995 is 1910 Class A5 Fowler road locomotive *Black Knight* (Works No 11111) at Engine Hill above Porthtowan, Cornwall.

LEONARD STANLEY Ready to take part in a local club run at Leonard Stanley, near Stroud, Gloucestershire, is 1913 Class D2 road locomotive *Activity*.

Left: **QUAINTON ROAD** 1917 Class R3 road locomotive *Kingfisher* stands at the Buckinghamshire Railway Centre in June 2001.

Above: **SUFFOLK** 1920 Class A9 road locomotive *Sir Douglas* runs through the spring countryside on the Great Eastern Road Run of April 1998.

EASTNOR Near this Herefordshire village in July 2001 is a 1928 Class B6 road locomotive hauling a transformer up Hollybush Hill.

TARRANT HINTON The Great Dorset Steam Fair in September 1999 saw this 1901 Fowler crane road locomotive in the heavy haulage arena.

Road rollers

KEMBLE Photographed at night in August 2004 outside one of the airfield's redundant hangars is a 1921 Class DN1 10-ton road roller in the company of a 1929 Ford Model AA. This rally will be held at South Cerney in the future.

CHOLSEY In August 2002, doing some rolling for real, is 1922 Class DH 10-ton road roller *Busy Bee*.

BIRMINGHAM 1923 Class DN1 8-ton road roller *Cavalier* is taking part in a road run in the Jewellery Quarter. The location is Mary Ann Street, near Snow Hill railway station. This road run was discontinued in the mid-1990s.

HANBURY On a road run at Hanbury, Worcestershire, in June 2003 is 1923 Class D5 12-ton road roller *Jessica*.

Left: **RUSHMOOR** This rally no longer takes place, but back in July 1992 one of the participants was 1927 Class T3B 6-ton road roller *Ruffle*.

Above: **LITTLE CHALFONT** At the completion of a road run amidst glorious autumn colours in October 2003, 1930 Class DNB 12-ton road roller *Arfur* enters Honors Yard at Little Chalfont.

AVONCROFT In the Worcestershire countryside near Bromsgrove we see 1931 Class DNA 8-ton road roller *Bacchus*.

Below: **BEAMISH** Seen at the Open Air Museum in May 2008 is 1931 Class DNA Fowler 10-ton road roller *Rambler*.

Right: **CLEEVE PRIOR** On a local road run at Cleeve Prior village, Worcestershire, in July 2003 is this 1937 Class T3A2 8-ton road roller.

Above: **GAMLINGAY** Another road run, this time the Bedfordshire Club event of May 2003; the engine is a 1927 Class DNA Fowler CRR (Convertible Road Roller) tractor, seen in its tractor form.

Previous page: **SHEFFIELD PARK** Outside Sheffield Park station on the Bluebell Railway in Sussex is 1895 Class A4 Fowler traction engine *Endurance.*

Above: **PICKERING** Photographed at this Yorkshire rally is 1907 Class BAA 'Colonial' traction engine *Geordie Lad.*

Right: **OLD WARDEN** 1909 Class R traction engine *Edna* is seen at the Bedfordshire Steam Rally.

AVONCROFT
At Avoncroft, Bromsgrove, Worcestershire, in April 1992 is 1911 traction engine *Elsa* of Class A8.

OWER *Volunteer* is another Class A8 traction engine from 1913, seen in Ower village near Southampton.

Left: **BELVOIR CASTLE** This May 2004 portrait is of 1920 Class T3 Fowler 'Tiger' tractor *Lord Doverdale*.

Right **REDDITCH** In May 2005 the National Traction Engine Trust training weekend was held at Davis's Yard, Astwood Bank, Redditch, Worcestershire, and running past the crushing plant is 1922 Class A9 traction engine *Tommy*

Showman's road locomotives

Left: **TARRANT HINTON** In the fairground at the Great Dorset Steam Fair in September 2002 is the appropriately named 1901 Class B5 road locomotive *Dawn of the Century*, with showman's fittings.

Above: **HIGHAM FERRERS** Seen at this rally in May 1992 is 1905 Class R1 showman's road locomotive *Sir John Fowler*.

RUSHMOOR In a fairground setting at this former rally in July 1995 is 1916 Class B showman's road locomotive *Carry-On.*

Above: **OLD WARDEN** At the Bedfordshire Steam Rally in September 2003, 1916 Class B showman's road locomotive *Valiant* is powering a fairground organ.

Right: **TARRANT HINTON** At the Great Dorset Steam Fair in September 1993 is 1919 Class T3 showman's 'Tiger' tractor *Firefly*.

Top right: **TALLINGTON** Beneath the Big Wheel at the Tallington Rally, an event since moved to Belvoir Castle, is 1920 Class R3 showman's road locomotive *Renown*.

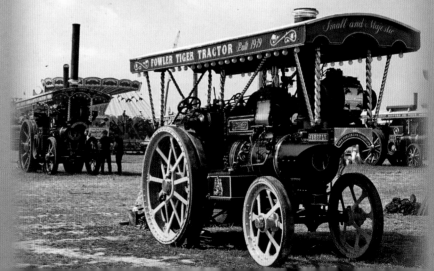

Top left: **STRATFORD-UPON-AVON** In June 1993, casting a smoke screen over the 'Coronation Speedway' at the Shire Horse Centre at Stratford-upon-Avon, since closed, is another 1920 R3, *Repulse*.

Left: **TARRANT HINTON** 1923 Class A9 showman's road locomotive *Pride of Shannon* poses at the Great Dorset Steam Fair in July 1999.

Above: **WELLAND RALLY** Next to some 1890s Gallopers at this Worcestershire rally in July 2006 is a 1931 Class DNB traction engine with showman's fittings. This shows the blurring between the various types of engine.

STANWAY The Fowler Class B6 'Super Lion' was the final flowering of road steam engineering. On a road run to Stanway House at the Gloucestershire Warwickshire Railway Steam & Vintage Gala is this 1932 example, *The Lion*.

KEMBLE *The Lion* is seen again at night in a fairground setting in August 2005 next to the 1893 Savage Gallopers with a Tidman steam centre engine.

ADDERBURY Another B6 'Super Lion', *Supreme* of 1934, is seen on a local road run near this Oxfordshire village in June 2004.

Ploughing engines

OLD WARDEN Arguably the best-known of all Fowler's products is the ploughing engine. Working at the Bedfordshire Steam Rally in September 2005 is 1870 example *Margaret*.

MUCH MARCLE With the plough in the foreground, 1873 ploughing engine *Noreen* is seen at the Marcle Rally in July 2002.

CHRIST'S HOSPITAL Fowler ploughing engines compete in the Steam Plough Club's Great Challenge of August 2009 at Christ's Hospital, Sussex. The first (*below*) is an 1875 example, the other (*right*) a year younger.

WEETING Coupled to a plough at the Weeting Rally is another 1876 ploughing engine.

PRESTON, KENT In October 2006 an 1877 ploughing engine is seen at Preston Services, Kent.

LOUGHBOROUGH In September 2006 the Steam Plough Club's Great Challenge was held at Loughborough. Here we see an 1884 ploughing engine at the event.

BRIDGNORTH Crossing the River Severn at Bridgnorth, Shropshire, on her way to Wolverhampton in May 2003 is a 1913 Class BB ploughing engine.

PRESTON, KENT 1914 Class K7 ploughing engine *The Steam Sapper* was photographed at Preston Services in October 2006.

WELLAND RALLY Another K7, 1916 ploughing engine *Linkey*, is doing what it was designed to do at the July 2000 event.

WADDESDON Two ploughing engines take part in ploughing demonstrations at this former Buckinghamshire rally in September 1991. The first (*main picture*) is 1916 Class T1 *Master John*, the other (*inset*) a 1917 Class AA6.

CHRIST'S HOSPITAL Back at the August 2009 Steam Plough Club's Great Challenge is another 1917 Class AA6, *Sir John (main picture)*, and 1918 Class BB1 *Berkshire Lady (inset)*.

AVON DASSETT
In July 2002 the Steam Plough Club's training event was held at this Warwickshire village. Here 1918 Class AA7 ploughing engine *Repulse* completes another strip.

BANBURY A fine portrait of a 1918 Class BB1 ploughing engine at the June 2003 rally.

HANBURY Another 1918 BB1 is on a local road run at Hanbury village, Worcestershire, in September 1997.

PORTHTOWAN High above Porthtowan beach in Cornwall, 1918 Class BB1 ploughing engine *Headland Beauty* is taking part in the West of England Steam Engine Society road run at Engine Hill.

LOUGHBOROUGH The September 2006
Steam Plough Club's Great Challenge also
featured 1919 Class BB1 *Black Prince*, seen here
hard at work.

WEETING 1919 Class BB1 *Churchill* demonstrates steam ploughing at the July 1999 rally.

Right: **LOUGHBOROUGH** Also taking part in the Steam Plough Club's Great Challenge of September 2006 was this 1922 Class Z7 ploughing engine, the most powerful of the class, most of which was repatriated from Senna Plantations, Mozambique.

AVON DASSETT Another 1922 Z7 is seen at work during the Steam Plough Club's training event.

WADDESDON A 1922 Z7 at the Waddesdon Rally of September 1992.

Main picture: **WEETING** 1926 Class K7 ploughing engine *Jack of Herts.*

Inset: **SOUTH CROXTON** Another K7, this one dating from 1929, poses at the Leicestershire meeting in August 2000.

CHRIST'S HOSPITAL A remarkable line-up of ploughing engines at the end of the day at the Steam Plough Club's Great Challenge in August 2009.

CHRIST'S HOSPITAL Attending that event was this 1926 R. J. H. Wilder ploughing engine, which was a rebuilt Fowler of 1869.

LOUGHBOROUGH The Steam Plough Club's Great Challenge of September 2006 featured this 1918 Class BB1 ploughing engine rebuilt with a Mercedes six-cylinder diesel engine.

Index

Build dates
1869. 48
1870 27
1873 28
1875 29
1876 30
1877 31
1884 32
1893 25
1895 16
1901 7, 20
1905 20
1907 16
1909 16
1910 3
1911 17
1913 4, 18, 33
1914 34
1916 21, 22, 35, 36
1917 5, 36, 37
1918 37, 38, 39, 40, 41, 48
1919 22, 42, 43
1920 5, 19, 22, 23
1921 8
1922 9, 19, 43, 44, 45
1923 10, 11, 23
1926 46, 48
1927 12, 14
1928 6
1929 8, 46
1930 12
1931 2, 13, 14, 23
1932 24
1934 2, 26
1937 2, 14

Engine names
Activity 4
Arfur 12
Bacchus 13
Berkshire Lady 37
Black Knight 3

Black Prince 42
Busy Bee 9
Carry-On 21
Cavalier 10
Churchill 43
Dawn of the Century 20
Edna 16
Elsa 17
Endurance 16
Firefly 22
Geordie Lad 16
Headland Beauty 41
Jack of Herts 46
Jessica 11
Kingfisher 5
Linkey 35
Lord Doverdale 19
Margaret 27
Master John 36
Noreen 28
Pendle Prince 2
Pride of Shannon 23
Rambler 14
Renown 22
Repulse 23, 38
Ruffle 12
Sir Douglas 5
Sir John 20, 37
Sir John Fowler 20
Supreme 26
The Lion 24, 25
The Steam Sapper 34
Tommy 19
Valiant 22
Volunteer 18

Image dates
September 1991 36
April 1992 17
May 1992 20
July 1992 12
September 1992. 45

June 1993 23
September 1993 22
September 1994 2
July 1995 21
August 1995 3
September 1997 40
April 1998 5
July 1999 23, 43
September 1999 7
July 2000 35
August 2000 46
June 2001 5
July 2001 6
July 2002 28, 38
August 2002 9
September 2002 20
May 2003 14, 33
June 2003 11, 39
July 2003 14
September 2003 22
October 2003 12
May 2004 19
June 2004 26
August 2004 8
May 2005 19
August 2005 25
September 2005 27
July 2006 23
September 2006 32, 42, 43, 48
October 2006 31, 34
May 2008 14
August 2009 29, 37, 47

Locations
ADDERBURY 26
AVONCROFT 13, 17
AVON DASSETT 38, 44
BANBURY 39
BEAMISH 14
BELVOIR CASTLE 19
BIRMINGHAM 10

BRIDGNORTH 33
CHOLSEY 9
CHRIST'S HOSPITAL 29, 37, 47, 48
CLEEVE PRIOR 14
EASTNOR 6
GAMLINGAY 14
HANBURY 11, 39
HIGHAM FERRERS 20
KEMBLE 8, 25
LEONARD STANLEY 4
LITTLE CHALFONT 12
LOUGHBOROUGH 32, 42, 43, 48
MUCH MARCLE 28
OLD WARDEN 16, 22, 27
OWER 18
PICKERING 16
PORTHTOWAN 3, 41
PRESTON, KENT 31, 34
QUAINTON ROAD 5
REDDITCH 19
RUSHMOOR 12, 21
SHEFFIELD PARK 16
SOUTH CROXTON 46
STANWAY 24
STRATFORD-UPON-AVON 23
SUFFOLK 5
TALLINGTON 22
TARRANT HINTON 2, 7, 20, 22, 23
WADDESDON 36, 45
WEETING 30, 43, 46
WELLAND RALLY 23, 35